NEW THEATRE, ST. MARTIN'S LA[

DONALD ALBERY
(for Donmar Productions Limited)

PRESENTS

RON MOODY

GEORGIA BROWN   PAUL WHITSUN-JONES

OLIVER!

ADAPTED FROM DICKEN'S " OLIVER TWIST "

WITH

HOPE JACKMAN   DANNY SEWELL
KEITH HAMSHERE   MARTIN HORSEY

BOOK, MUSIC AND LYRICS BY
LIONEL BART

Directed by PETER COE

Designed by SEAN KENNY

Musical Director MARCUS DODS

Musical arrangements by ERIC ROGERS

Lighting by JOHN WYCKHAM

VOCAL SCORE
(by JOHN EVANS)

LAKEVIEW MUSIC PUBLISHING CO. LTD.
SUITE 2.07, PLAZA 535 KING'S ROAD, LONDON SW10 0SZ

Sole selling agents: MUSIC SALES LTD., 8/9 Frith Street, London W1V 5TZ.

Printed in England by Caligraving Limited Thetford Norfolk

First performance at the New Theatre, St. Martin's Lane, June 30, 1960

OLIVER!

THE CAST
(in order of appearance)

OLIVER TWIST .. .. KEITH HAMSHERE

WORKHOUSE BOYS AND FAGIN'S GANG .. .. CHARLES BROWN, JONATHAN COLLINS, PETER EVELEIGH, PATRICK FURLOUGH, MICHAEL GOODMAN, CLIVE GREEN, BRIAN LEWIS, DENNIS MALLARD, STEPHEN MARRIOTT, BARRY NEWNHAM, NICHOLAS NORMAN, TONY ROBINSON, ALAN SHORTLAND, ROYSTON THOMAS

MR. BUMBLE .. .. PAUL WHITSUN-JONES

WIDOW CORNEY .. .. HOPE JACKMAN

MR. SOWERBERRY .. .. BARRY HUMPHRIES

MRS. SOWERBERRY.. .. .. SONIA FRASER

CHARLOTTE .. .. APPLE BROOK

NOAH CLAYPOLE .. .. TREVOR RAY

THE ARTFUL DODGER .. .. MARTIN HORSEY

LONDONERS .. SALLY BITTON, ANNA LEROY, JEAN ANN PAGE, JANET PATE, ELIZABETH PERRY, JULIA SUTTON, DAVID BEAUMONT, JONATHAN BROMLEY, ERIC HOLMES, ROB INGLIS, ROBERT KEMP, LARRY OAKS, STANLEY PRICE, BRIAN SCOTT, JIM SPARROW

FAGIN .. .. RON MOODY

NANCY .. .. GEORGIA BROWN

BET .. .. DIANE GRAY

MR. BROWNLOW .. .. GEORGE BISHOP

BILL SYKES .. .. DANNY SEWELL

MRS. BEDWIN .. .. MADELEINE NEWBURY

DR. GRIMWIG .. .. CLAUDE JONES

OLD SALLY.. .. .. BETTY TURNER

OLIVER!

MUSICAL CONTENTS

SYNOPSIS OF SCENES

The place is London. The time about 1850.

ACT I

Scene 1.   The Workhouse—early evening

Scene 2.   The Workhouse Parlour—later (into Street)

Scene 3.   The Undertaker's

Scene 4.   The Undertaker's—Next morning

Scene 5.   Paddington Green—Morning, a week later.

Scene 6.   The Thieves' Kitchen—Later (into Street)

ACT II

Scene 1.   The " Three Cripples " a Public House in Clerkenwell—The following
            evening (into Street)

Scene 2.   The Brownlows' Morning Room—Two weeks later

Scene 3.   The Thieves' Kitchen—(ending in Street Area)

Scene 4.   The Workhouse—A few days later (into Street)

Scene 5.   The Brownlows' House—(into Street)

Scene 6.   London Bridge—Midnight (using Street Area)

FINALE

London Bridge

OLIVER!

LIONEL BART

OVERTURE AND OPENING SCENE

No 1

Act I

CHORUS– (with Oliver and 1st, 2nd, 3rd and 4th Solo Boys)
"FOOD, GLORIOUS FOOD"

Oliver

Oliver

4

Oliver

6

Oliver

Oliver

8

Oliver

Oliver

The boy on Oliver's right bangs his empty bowl on that of the boy on his right, who in turn picks the two bowls up and bangs them on that of the boy on his right, and so on round the table until the pile of bowls reaches Oliver who snatches his away just in time

Oliver rises to his feet, advances, bowl in hand, towards Mr. Bumble— and stops in front of him

OLIVER *(spoken)*
Please sir, I want some more

Oliver

Nº 3

CHORUS- (with Mr. Bumble and Widow Corney)
"OLIVER"

Oliver is forced to his knees in front of
Mr. Bumble and the boys gather round
him in a mocking circle.

Oliver

14

W. Corney and Mr. Bumble　　　**Mr. Bumble**

O - li - ver!　O - li - ver!　Nev-er be-fore has a　boy want-ed more.

W. Corney and Mr. Bumble　　**W. Corney**　　　**Mr. Bumble**

O - li - ver!　O - li - ver!　Won't ask for more when he　knows what's in store. There's a

Mr BU　　soo - ty chim - ney,　long ov-er-due for a　sweep-ing out.＿Which we'll

Mr BU　　push him　up,　and　one day next year with the　rats he'll be creep-ing out.

Oliver

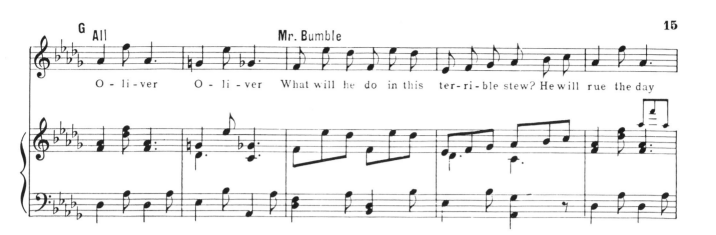

O - li - ver   O - li - ver   What will he do in this ter-ri-ble stew? He will rue the day

some - bo - dy named him   O - li - ver!

W. CORNEY (*Spoken*) (*to pauper assistants.*) Lock him up! Find his belongings and bring him back when you've done.
(*to the rest of the boys*) To bed all of you.

No. 3a

END OF SCENE

Presto

The boys are hustled off and Mr. Bumble and Widow Corney retire to the Widow's parlour for tea.

Oliver

DUET– (Widow Corney and Mr. Bumble)
"I SHALL SCREAM"

Mr. Bumble puts down his teacup and kisses Widow Corney

Cue: W. CORNEY "Mr Bumble, I shall scream!"

Allegretto ♩= 100

Mr. Bumble

No you would-n't. Heigh – ho, If I want-ed some-thing

spe-cial, then you could-n't say "No" Did I near-ly catch you

smil-ing? Yes I did and it's be – guil-ing. If your hand is close I'll

press it. Yes you like it, come con – fess it! Yes, you do. No, I

W. Corney

Oliver

Oliver

18

Oliver

Oliver

Oliver

Oliver

SONG – (Mr Bumble)
"BOY FOR SALE"

Oliver

No 6

TRIO – (Mr Sowerberry, Mrs Sowerberry and Mr Bumble)
"THAT'S YOUR FUNERAL"

Oliver is standing under an undertaker's sign wearing a top hat
Cue: Mrs SOWERBERRY: Can you keep that expression for a long time, boy, with a crowd watching you?
OLIVER: Yes ma'am I think so.

Oliver

Oliver

Oliver

Oliver

Nº 6a   COFFIN MUSIC

Cue: Mrs SOWERBERRY: Now then Oliver Twist you can sleep here under the counter. You don't mind sleeping among coffins I suppose. But it doesn't much matter whether you do or don't, you can't sleep no where else

She takes the lamp and shuts Oliver in the shop

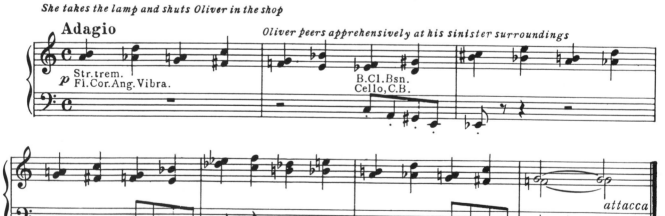

Oliver

№ 7

SONG – (Oliver)

"WHERE IS LOVE?"

Oliver

Oliver

NEXT MORNING

№ 8

Oliver rises, crosses to the counter and goes to sleep underneath it

Noah Claypole arrives at the street door and bangs and kicks it

Meno mosso ♩ = 112

B NOAH (off) Open the door will yer?

OLIVER: I will directly sir (undoing the chain and turning the key)

NOAH:(through the keyhole) Are you the new boy?

OLIVER: Yes sir

NOAH:(still outside) How old are yer?

OLIVER: Thirteen sir

Dialogue continues

Nº 8a

THE FIGHT

Cue: NOAH: A regular right down bad 'un.
And its a good thing she died when
she did or she'd have been doing hard.
labour in prison as like as not.

*Oliver jumps up and throws
Noah over the counter and a
struggle follows.*

NOAH – *(shouts)* He'll murder me! Charlotte! Missis!
Tnis here new boy's a murderin' of

me! Help! Help! He's gorn *mad!* Char-*LOTTE !!*

CHARLOTTE *(off)*
What's up?

MRS SOWERBERRY *(off)*
What on earth can be happening?
Coming, coming, Noah.

*Charlotte and
Mrs Sowerberry enter*

Charlotte seizes Oliver

CHARLOTTE: Oh you horrid wretch!
You little ungrateful murderous

villain

*Charlotte and Mrs Sowerberry take
an arm each and shake Oliver vigorously.
Noah gets up and pummel him from behind. They finally drag Oliver to a coffin, push him in, close the*
W.W.

Oliver

Oliver

OLIVER'S ESCAPE

Cue: MRS SOWERBERRY — Well, and what if he did,
you little ungrateful wretch? She probably
deserved what was said and worse.

OLIVER — She didn't !

MRS SOWERBERRY — She did ! ,

OLIVER — Its a lie

*Mrs Sowerberry utters a shriek and
falls into the coffin which closes.
The others rush to help her.*

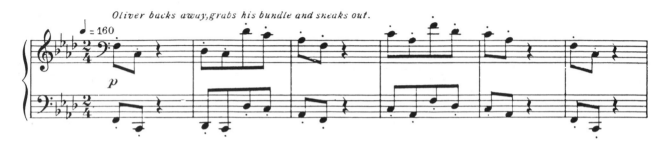

Oliver backs away, grabs his bundle and sneaks out.

NOAH — He's gone !   MRS SOWERBERRY — Who's gone ?   CHARLOTTE — Oliver- he's run off !

MR SOWERBERRY — Five pounds worth - run off ? *Five* pounds of mine ? Run off ? After him !

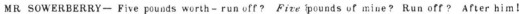

MR BUMBLE *(to Mrs Sowerberry as he runs)* Meat, madam ! Meat.

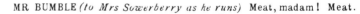

(There is chaos as they all clamber for the shop door)

Oliver

Oliver has eluded his

pursuers and appears, breathless, at the top of a flight of stairs in Paddington Green.

Moderato
OLIVER *(humming to himself)*

Oliver

SONG — (The Artful Dodger, Oliver and Chorus)
"CONSIDER YOURSELF"

Cue: DODGER — Come to think of it— I ain't got no intimate
friends still what's the difference, me old pork
sausage, you're coming along with me.

OLIVER — Are you sure Mr Fagin won't mind ?

DODGER — Mind ?

Oliver

Oliver

DOD

Then the drinks are on the house! _____ Con-

W.W.

D

DOD

-si-der your-self our mate. We don't want to have no

Str.

DOD

fuss, For af - ter some con - si - de-ra - tion we can state Con -

W.W.

(Dodger illustrates various Cockney actions which Oliver tries to emulate.)

E

Oliver

DOD

-si-der your-self one of us! Con - si-der your-self At

W.W.

Tutti

f

Bsn.
Cello

Oliver

Oliver

42

Oliver

(l'istesso)

(C.B.)

Oliver

Oliver

Oliver

Oliver

Oliver

ENCORE — (Chorus)
"CONSIDER YOURSELF"

The children proceed towards the thieves' kitchen as the crowd gradually disperses singing off

Oliver

49

Oliver

50

Oliver

Nº 11   SONG—(Fagin, with the Boys)
"PICK A POCKET OR TWO"

FAGIN: I suppose a laundry would be a very nice thing indeed but our line of business pays a little better— don't it boys?

BOYS: Not 'arf!

Oliver

While Fagin attends to the eye, the boy removes Fagin's watch.

what he took Cha-ri-ty's fine, Sub-scibe to mine Get out and pick a poc-ket or

two. You've got to pick a poc-ket or two, boys. You've got to pick a poc-ket or

two Ro-bin Hood was far too good, You've got to pick a poc-ket or

Three boys attract Fagin's attention to something in the sky. As he gazes

two Take a tip From Bill Sykes— He can whip What he likes

upward the smallest boy swoops under Fagin's cloak to remove his pocket handkerchief.

I — re-call He start-ed small, He had to pick a poc-ket or two! You've

Oliver

54

FAGIN (spoken) Put 'em back in the box.

The boys return the articles

they have stolen to the box with the exception of one, whom Fagin sees out of the corner of his eye.   FAGIN–all of 'em.

The boy shamefacedly

returns a spectacle case to the box.

FAGIN Come 'ere–(Pats boy on head)–What a crook!

FAGIN: Just do everything that Dodger and Charlie do. Make 'em your models, my dear, especially Dodger.   He's going to be a right little Bill Sykes!

Now then, is my handkerchief protruding from my pocket?

OLIVER: Yes sir I can just see the corner

FAGIN: See if you can take it out without my feeling it–like you saw the others do.

Fagin (sings) Oliver tries unsuccessfully to steal the

Rum tum tum.   Rum tum tum.

Oliver

№ 12　　　　　　　　　　　INTERMEZZO

№ 13　　　　DUET—(Nancy and Bet with the Boys)
"IT'S A FINE LIFE"

Cue: FAGIN: Well today's yer birthday—wash!
Oliver moves over to the corner and Fagin returns the box to its hiding place
NANCY (off.) Plummy and Slam!

All the boys wake up
Nancy enters with Bet
FAGIN: The ladies! Wake up boys. The ladies are here.
NANCY: We'll have less of that if you don't mind.
　　　　Where's the gin!
FAGIN: All in moderation my dear. Too much gin can
　　　　be a dangerous thing for a pure young girl.
NANCY: And what's wrong with a bit of danger, then
　　　　Mr. Fagin? After all, that's the only bit of ex-
　　　　citement we have isn't it? And who would
　　　　deny us this small pleasure?

Oliver

60

Oliver

Oliver

Oliver

№ 14   ENSEMBLE— (The Artful Dodger, Nancy, Oliver, Bet, Fagin and the Boys)
"I'D DO ANYTHING"

Cue: NANCY: Have you seen the way them quality gentlemen treats their ladies?
DODGER: Yuss!
NANCY: Shall we show them?
FAGIN: Go on, Nancy, give us a free show on the stage
NANCY: It's all bowing and hats off
and....

Gavotte (♩ = 120)

DODGER: Don't let your petticoats dangle in the mud my darling. NANCY: And "I'll go last" DODGER: No I'll

Fl.

Vln.Cl.
Br.sust.
Bsn.Cello(Glock.)
mf

go last. NANCY: No I'll go last.   *Dodger sings this send up on the gentry* **A** Dodger

I'd   do   a-ny-thing   For   etc.

Fl.8va
Ob.
tr
W.W.

Vln.
Br.sust.

DOD
you,   dear,   a-ny-thing—   For   you   mean   ev'-ry-thing   To   me

W.W.Glock.

B

DOD
I know that   I'd   go   a-ny-where   For   your   smile,   a-ny-where—   For

W.W.

Vln.
Br.sust.

Oliver

Oliver

E Oliver *Oliver and Bet imitate Dodger and Nancy*

I'd do a-ny-thing For you, dear, a-ny-thing— For you mean

ev-'ry-thing To me._____ I know that I'd go a-ny-where For

your smile, a-ny-where— For your smile ev-'ry-where I'd see_____

Bet G   **Oliver**   **Bet**   **Oliver**   **Bet**

Would you lace my shoe? A-ny-thing! Paint your face bright blue? A-ny-thing! Catch a

Oliver

Kan-ga-roo? A-ny-thing! Go to Tim-buc-too? And back a-gain! I'd risk

ev'ry-thing For one kiss— ev'ry-thing— Yes I'd do a-ny-thing A-ny-thing?

A-ny-thing for you!

Oliver

Oliver

No 15

SONG— (Fagin, The Artful Dodger and the Boys)
"BE BACK SOON"

Oliver

Oliver

thieves. Whip-it quick and be back soon There's a six-pence here for twen-ty Ain't

that a love-ly tune Be back soon. Our pock-ets'll hold a

Dodger D

watch of gold that chimes up-on the ho-ur A wal-let fat, an old man's hat, the

1st Solo Boy **2nd Solo Boy** **Dodger**

crown jew-els from the Tow - er We know the Bow Street Run-ners But they don't know this

All the Boys **Dodger**

tune So long, fare thee well, Pip, pip, cheer-i - o We'll be back soon _____ Cheer-i -

All the Boys **Fagin**

Oliver

72

Oliver

Oliver

Oliver

No 15a

CAPTURE OF OLIVER

Oliver

76

Oliver

As Oliver stands transfixed, suspicion centres on him and he is encircled

C **Presto** ♩ = 160

D *Oliver makes a run for it pursued by the crowd*

Oliver

78

Oliver

Oliver is encircled again
He makes a break for it and is — struck on the head
Oliver falls down unconscious.
He is lifted by two Bow Street runners
Mr Brownlow identifies him with a nod
Curtain

Cym. l.v.

End of Act I

Oliver

Act II

SONG – (Nancy and Chorus)
"OOM - PAH - PAH"

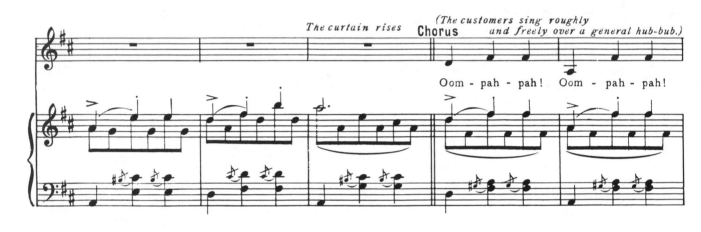

Oliver

82

Oliver

When they hear Oom - pah - pah! _____ Mis - ter Per-cy

Snod - grass would of - ten have the odd glass—But ne - ver when he thought a - ny -

-bo - dy could see. Sec - ret - ly he'd buy it, And drink it on the

qui - et, And dream he was an earl with a girl on each knee!

Oliver

Oliver

86

Oliver

Oliver

88

Nancy *sings*

There's a lit-tle dit-ty They're sing-ing in the ci-ty Es-pesh-ly when they've

Chorus

Oom-pah-pah! Oom-pah-pah! That's how it goes. Oom-pah-pah!

NAN

been on the gin or the beer. If you've got the pa-tience, Your

CHO

Oom-pah-pah! Ev-'ry-one knows. They all sup-pose What they

NAN

own i-ma-gi-na-tions Will tell you just ex-act-ly what you want to

CHO

want to sup-pose. When they hear Oom-pah-pah!

Oliver

Oliver

SONG— (Bill Sykes)
"MY NAME"

Bill Sykes enters and strikes the floor with his cudgel to gain attention.
Silence follows.

Cue: OLD HAG *(whispers loudly)* Bill Sykes!

Strong men trem-ble when they hear it!

Sykes slowly descends the stairs into the tavern

They've got cause e-nough to fear it! It's much black-er than they smear it!

No-bo-dy men-tions... My name! Rich men hold their five-pound notes out Saves me

emp-ty-ing their coats out They know I could tear their throats out Just to live up to My name!

Oliver

Oliver

Oliver

He could take my name in vain   Poor bloke   Shame e was so green   Nev-er was he seen a-

-gain!   Once bad, what's the good of turn-ing   In hell!   I'll be there a burn-ing

Sykes walks around the saloon baring his fist at one and all, daring them to answer.

Mean while,   think of what I'm earn-ing   All on ac-count of...   My name!

(jubilantly)

What is it?___   What is it?___   What is it?___   My   name!

Str. Br.   W.W.   Tutti *ff*   *Dialogue*

Oliver

SONG— (Nancy)
"AS LONG AS HE NEEDS ME"

*(The hurdy-gurdy can still be heard outside and is
interrupted by the first chord of the song.)*

Oliver

Oliver

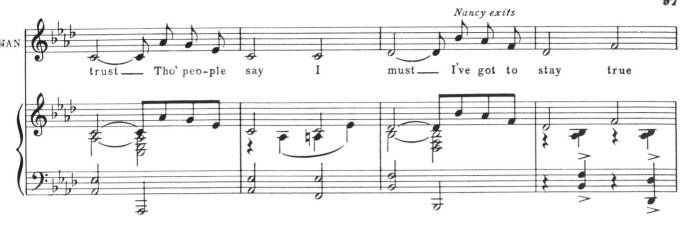

Nancy exits

trust — Tho' peo-ple say I must — I've got to stay true

ten.ten.ten.

just ____ as long as he needs me ____

Tutti

f

attacca

Nº 19   CHANGE OF SCENE

♩ = 76

Cor A. Hn. Vln.

The scene changes to a bedroom in Mr Brownlow's house

p

Cl.

Bsn. Cello

Glock.
Pno.

Trom.

attacca

Oliver

Nº 20

REPRISE— (Mrs Bedwin)
"WHERE IS LOVE?"

Nº 21

ENSEMBLE— (Oliver, Street Criers and Chorus)
"WHO WILL BUY?"

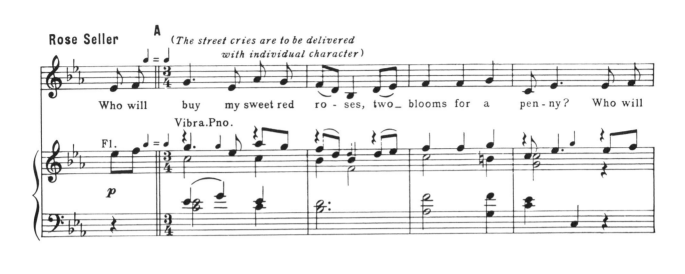

Oliver

Oliver

Oliver

Oliver

Cue MR BROWNLOW
Now we shall see, Mrs Bedwin. Ten minutes!
Oliver goes out into the street which is full of street criers and passers by (gentry.)

Oliver

Oliver

Nº 22

CHANGE OF SCENE

Cue: SYKES: He's nothing but a thief and a vagabond.

Oliver

№ 23 REPRISE —(Nancy, Bill Sykes, Fagin and The Artful Dodger)
"IT'S A FINE LIFE"

Cue: NANCY: Civil words, yes, you deserve them from me. I thieved when I was half his age and for twelve years since.

SYKES: Well, if you have, it's your living.

Oliver

Oliver

SONG—(Fagin)
"REVIEWING THE SITUATION"

Cue: FAGIN:*(spoken) to Sykes:* Look after her, Bill.*(Sykes follows Nancy off)*
       to Dodger: Look after him, Dodger — *(Dodger takes Oliver off)*
       to Audience: —and I'll look after meself.

Oliver

Oliver

Oliver

Oliver

Oliver

Oliver

Oliver

*Footnote: The lower line of words was used in the original production at The New Theatre, and at this point the scene began to change, Fagin returning to the fireplace to count his money as the revolve took him off.

120

CHANGE OF SCENE

*The scene continues to change
into the workhouse parlour*

Mr Bumble enters
alla marcia

*Mr Bumble sits on
the parlour steps*

Dialogue

CHANGE OF SCENE

Mr Bumble makes to exit, cuffing a small boy who has been laughing at his scene with Widow Corney (Boy exits crying)

Adagio

The lights come up on the back room of the workhouse where old Sally lies dying

*Repeat ad lib.
until Sally dies*

Segue

Oliver

No 25   REPRISE— (Widow Corney and Mr Bumble)
"OLIVER"

Cue: WIDOW CORNEY: We must retrieve that boy Mr Bumble
　　　Mr BUMBLE: We must indeed ma'am, we must indeed

Oliver

N⁰ 26

REPRISE— (Nancy)
"AS LONG AS HE NEEDS ME"

Cue: NANCY: Then tonight, between eleven and the time the clock strikes twelve,
I will walk on London Bridge — and I will bring Oliver!

She leaves Mr Brownlow's house and enters the street

O'liver

124

Oliver

no - one _____ to take his part _____ I'll take his

part, Bill _____ but cross my heart _____ I won't be -

-tray your trust ___ Tho' peo-ple say I must ___ I've got to stay true

just _____ as long as Bill needs me. _____

Nancy exits

Tutti

End of Scene

Oliver

Nº 27   LONDON BRIDGE

Oliver

D Presto

Sykes grabs Oliver and drags him away
towards the thieves' kitchen

W.W.
Xylo.

Mr Brownlow catches sight of
Sykes disappearing round a corner

Mr Brownlow sees

Nancy's body

He calls for help

F Mr Brownlow reaches
the body

The night watchman reappears with
another couple, carrying lanterns

G

NIGHT WATCHMAN: Murder!
He exits ringing his bell

*Sykes reaches the thieves' kitchen
and hammers on the door*
SYKES: Let me in, Fagin, let me in!   *Fagin lets
them in*   *A crowd gathers round Mr Brownlow and the
body*

Oliver

130

BOW ST. RUNNER *(to crowd)*: Stand back! Stand back
(to Mr. Brownlow): Can you tell us what happened?
MR. BROWNLOW: Well, I came here to meet this poor creature and,
as I crossed the bridge I saw somebody disap-
pearing rapidly in the opposite direction.
BOW ST. RUNNER: Can you tell me what he looked like, sir?
MR. BROWNLOW: He was a broad shouldered heavily built man.
BOW ST. RUNNER: Anything else?
MR. BROWNLOW: He wore a blue coat and a tall hat.

Oliver

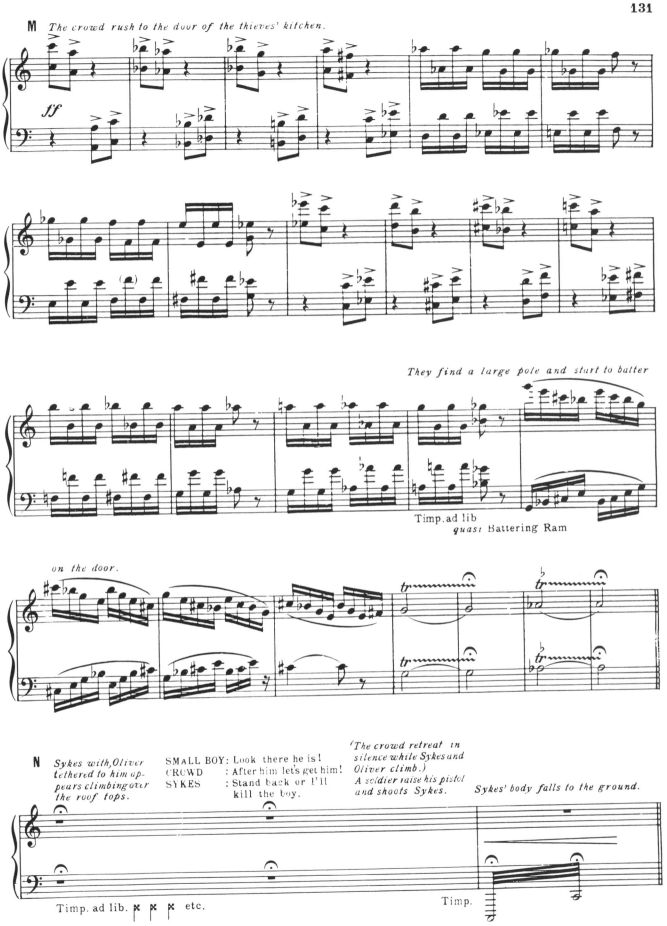

M *The crowd rush to the door of the thieves' kitchen.*

They find a large pole and start to batter

Timp. ad lib
quasi Battering Ram

on the door.

N *Sykes with, Oliver tethered to him appears climbing over the roof tops.*

SMALL BOY: Look there he is!
CROWD   : After him let's get him!
SYKES   : Stand back or I'll kill the boy.

(The crowd retreat in silence while Sykes and Oliver climb.)
A soldier raise his pistol and shoots Sykes.

Sykes' body falls to the ground.

Timp. ad lib. etc.

Timp.

Oliver

Oliver is helped to safety and taken to Mr Brownlow.
(The crowd roar approval)

The crowd pick up the pole and start to batter down the door again

Timp.ad lib.

They come out leading Dodger.
DODGER: Do you realise who you are a-laying your hands on? Assault and battery that is what it is! Wakin' a respeckable man up in the early hours of the morning. Shame on you! Shame on you! If only my attorney was here — but he's having breakfast with the Vice President of the House of Commons.

The door gives way and the Bow St. Runners enter the thieves' kitchen.

Timp. ✗ ✗ ✗ etc.

Oliver

The 1st Bow St. Runner hauls Dodger off.

The 2nd Bow St.Runner emerges

1st MAN : It's Fagin's money? 2nd MAN: Where's Fagin, then?
3rd MAN: Come out Fagin!   CROWD: We want Fagin!
We want Fagin!(etc.)

3rd BOW ST. RUNNER : There's nothing else in the place.
It's empty now.

CROWD : If Fagin ain't here there's only one place he can
be – The Three Cripples! Come on!

carrying Fagin's box of loot and exits.

attacca

No 28

REPRISE – (Fagin)
"REVIEWING THE SITUATION"

The crowd rush off shouting.
Mr Brownlow leads Oliver away.

Mrs Bedwin appears.
Oliver runs to meet her.
Fl. Cl.
Str.

MR BROWNLOW : Come, Oliver, we'll take
you home now. (All exit)

Fagin emerges
from under the
bridge recess.
Solo Vln.

Oliver

Fagin

Can

a piacere

dim. - - p

FAG: some-bo-dy change? It's pos-si-ble. May-be it's strange but it's pos-si-ble. All my

Vln. (8va)

Vln.

colla voce

FAG: bo-som com-pan-ions and trea-sures, I've left them be - hind. I'll

FAG: turn a leaf o-ver and who can tell what I may find? _____

Cor A.
Hn.

p

Alone and friendless, Fagin walks over the bridge off into the dawn

Maestoso

CURTAIN

Tutti

ff

Segue

Oliver

Finale

REPRISE — (Boys)
"FOOD, GLORIOUS FOOD"

Oliver

№ 30

REPRISE-- (Company)
"CONSIDER YOURSELF"

Oliver

ALL: Con - si-der your-self part of the fur - ni-ture There is-n't a lot

ALL: to spare Who cares what ev-er we've got we

ALL: share If it should chance to be we should see some hard-er days. Emp-ty lard-er days

ALL: Why grouse? Al-ways a chance we'll meet some-bo-dy to foot the bill

ALL: Then the drinks are on the house Con -

Oliver

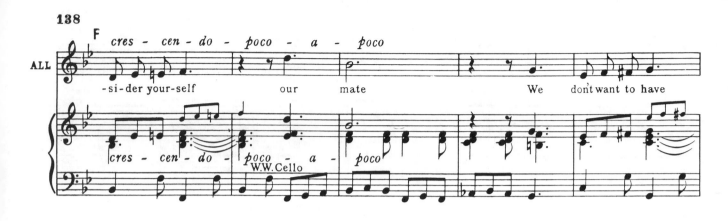

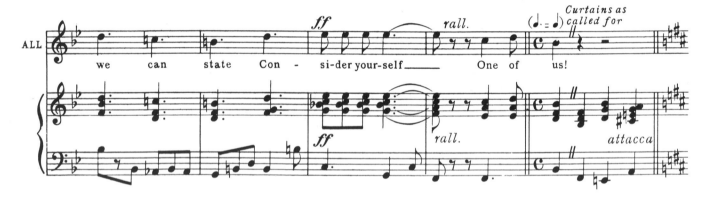

Nº 31   REPRISE— (Oliver and Company)
"I'D DO ANYTHING"

Oliver

Nº 32   EXIT MUSIC

Oliver

Oliver